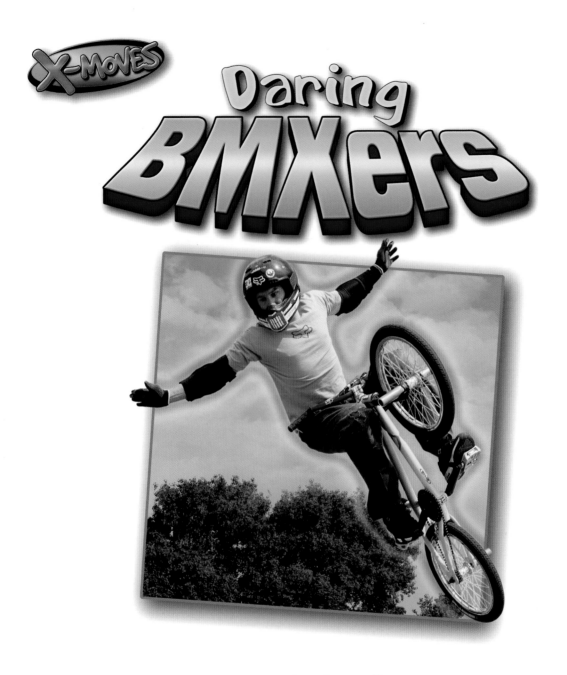

X-MOVES

Daring BMXers

by Michael Sandler

Consultant: David Fiedler
Editor of bicycling.about.com

BEARPORT
PUBLISHING

New York, New York

Credits

Cover and Title Page, © Mark Mainz/Getty Images for T-Mobile; TOC, © Vince Clements/Shutterstock; 4L, © Icon Sports Media; 4R, © Shotfile/Ultimate Group,LLC/Alamy; 5, © Icon Sports Media; 6, © Schwinn via Getty Images; 7, © James Cassimus/cassimusfotos; 8, © Gork Barrette/Redline Bicycles; 9, © Jeff Siner/Charlotte Observer/MCT/Landov; 10, © Chad Phillips/Digital Light Source, Inc; 11, © Tamás Olajos/overtoner.com; 12, © Jeff Zielinski/JeffZielinskiPhoto.com; 13, © Steve Boyle/NewSport/Corbis; 14, © Chad Phillips/Digital Light Source, Inc; 15, © Fat Tony; 16, © Cody York/ESPN Action Sports; 17, © Fat Tony; 18, © AP Images/Ivan Sekretarev; 19, © Carl De Souza/AFP/Getty Images; 20, © Max Breslow/maxbreslow.com; 21T, © Tony Donaldson/Icon SMI; 21B, Michael Buckner/Getty Images; 22L, © Fat Tony; 22R, © Anne-Marie Sorvin/Icon SMI.

Publisher: Kenn Goin
Senior Editor: Lisa Wiseman
Creative Director: Spencer Brinker
Photo Researcher: Daniella Nilva

Helmets are a rider's most important piece of safety gear. If you try BMX racing, or any form of BMX riding, wear one. It's the only way to ride.

Library of Congress Cataloging-in-Publication Data

Sandler, Michael, 1965-
  Daring BMXers / by Michael Sandler.
     p. cm. — (X-moves)
  Includes bibliographical references and index.
  ISBN-13: 978-1-59716-952-3 (library binding)
  ISBN-10: 1-59716-952-8 (library binding)
  1. Bicycle motocross— Juvenile literature. 2. Cyclists— United States— Biography— Juvenile literature. I. Title.
GV1049.3.S33 2010
796.6'2— dc22

2009019769

For more information, write to Bearport Publishing Company, Inc., 101 Fifth Avenue, Suite 6R, New York, New York 10003. Printed in the United States of America.

10 9 8 7 6 5 4 3 2 1

Contents

Landing the Trick 4

BMX Begins 6

BMX Racing 8

Freestyle 10

Park and Vert 12

Street and Dirt 14

The X Games 16

The Olympics 18

Flying High 20

BMX 101 22

Glossary 23

Bibliography 24

Read More 24

Learn More Online 24

Index 24

Landing the Trick

BMX star Kevin Robinson had worked for years on the double **flair**. Kevin had invented the trick, but he had never been able to land it.

Too many times, he'd sped up a **halfpipe**, spun upside down, and crashed. **Wiping out** wasn't fun. When it happened, he always said to himself, *Let me get out of this alive!*

Now, in front of a huge **X Games** crowd, Kevin was trying again. He rode into the air, did one backflip, then another, and made a perfect landing. "The first time in history," screamed the TV announcer, "that's a double flair!"

A halfpipe

A flair is a backflip with a corkscrew-like spin. In a double flair, the rider does two backflips while spiraling through the air.

Other riders celebrated with Kevin after he landed his double flair.

Kevin's double flair won him the gold medal for Best Trick at the 2006 Summer X Games.

BMX Begins

What does BMX stand for? It's short for "bicycle motocross." Motocross is a sport where riders race their motorcycles around dirt courses, making sharp turns and jumping over steep hills. Back in the 1960s, kids looked at motocross and thought: Why not race bikes the same way? Soon, a new sport was born.

The first BMX tracks were in Southern California. Early riders rode ordinary bikes such as Schwinn Sting-Rays with raised handlebars. As the sport grew, companies began making special bikes just for BMX. With small 20-inch (51-cm) wheels, **knobby** dirt tires, and light, strong frames, these bikes could turn quickly and handle the jumps easily.

The Schwinn Sting-Ray

A BMX bike race during the late 1970s in California

On July 10, 1969, a bicycle race was held at the newly built Palms Park in Santa Monica, California. Many consider it the world's first BMX race.

BMX Racing

BMX races are fast, furious, and very, very short—usually less than a quarter mile (.4 km). Each **heat**, called a moto, is a single lap around a track. Up to eight riders burst from the starting gate in a group. Each tries to gain the lead, handle hills and turns, and avoid "crashing out." A moto ends with a wild **sprint** to the finish line.

The top finishers in each moto move up to the next round to race again. After several more rounds, the remaining riders race a final moto. This one, called the Main, decides the overall winner of the competition.

BMX riders at the starting gate

Champion racer Mike Day (# 365) leads the pack over a jump during a moto in the BMX quarter finals at the 2008 Olympics.

From start to finish, a BMX moto usually lasts less than one minute.

Freestyle

BMX started with racing, but soon a different kind of riding grew out of it—freestyle. Freestyle means using BMX bikes to do tricks off the track. From the start, BMX racers liked to do tricks on their bikes between races. They popped wheelies or rode standing on the seats of their bikes. Each rider would show off, trying to outdo the others.

Since a track wasn't needed and a rider could work on tricks anywhere, freestyle grew quickly. Today it has different forms: flatland, park, **vert**, street, and dirt.

A freestyle BMX rider performing a trick

Flatland rider
Matthias Dandois

Flatland was the first type of freestyle. It means doing tricks on the ground—on a flat smooth surface. Flatland riders flip their bikes into strange positions, spinning and balancing on one wheel. They do this while standing on pegs that come out of the bike's wheels.

Park and Vert

Park freestylers do their tricks in skate parks. Like skateboarders, they ride up curved ramps and jump over boxes. They do tricks like feebles, hopping the front tire onto an **obstacle**—usually a wall or a box. Then they slide along, **grinding** their back pegs against the obstacle's edge.

Vert riders speed up ramps, launch into the air, and then do spins, flairs, **tailwhips**, and other flying tricks. Mat "The **Condor**" Hoffman and Dave Mirra were two of the early vert kings. Mat hit the first ever 900—two and a half full spins of the bike. Then after 13 years of trying, in 2002, he did the impossible, a no-hands 900!

BMXer Eric Hough does a wall grind.

Dave Mirra performing a tailwhip

Vert specialists use giant ramps for their tricks, bigger than those found in normal skate parks.

Street and Dirt

It's no surprise that street is the most popular form of freestyle. Head outside and the whole world seems like a skate park to BMXers. For street riders such as Eric Holley, there are plenty of objects to use for grinds, **taps**, or other tricks. A curb, a ledge, a set of stairs, or the walls around parking lots work just fine!

A dirt specialist such as Corey Bohan, on the other hand, skips the concrete street. He rides trails filled with dirt mounds like those found on BMX tracks. There is no racing involved. Instead, riders focus on jumping over the mounds smoothly and doing all the tricks that they can.

BMXers often use a wall to help them perform tricks.

Corey Bohan does a one-footed turn off of a mound of dirt.

Dirt riders usually build their own jumps in parks or on vacant land. They work together to shape mounds of dirt into perfect hills.

The X Games

Each style of BMX has its own competitions. One of the biggest events for freestylers is the X Games. In 2008, there were contests for Vert, Street, Park, and **Big Air**.

Riders win by doing the toughest, most creative tricks and getting the highest scores from the judges. For example, in Park, riders take turns doing runs around the course. They have 30 seconds each to show off their wildest moves. Venezuela's Daniel Dhers won the 2008 gold medal for Park with a run that included double tailwhips and a **540 barspin**.

Van Homan during the BMX Street Finals at the 2008 Summer X Games

Daniel Dhers during the 2008 Summer X Games SuperPark competition

The first time the X Games had a park-style competition was in 2008. The event was called SuperPark.

The Olympics

For BMX racers, the Olympic Games are now the top competition of all. BMX racing became an Olympic sport at the 2008 games in Beijing, China.

The track at Beijing was one of the finest ever built. The downhill start was a **massive** ramp as tall as a three-story building. By the time the racers reached the bottom, they were moving as fast as cars on a highway.

Americans took three of the first six BMX Olympic medals, with Mike Day and Donny Robinson winning the silver and the bronze in the men's competition. Jill Kintner, meanwhile, took the bronze in women's BMX.

Jill Kintner races toward a bronze medal at the 2008 Olympics in Beijing.

Racers during the BMX finals at the 2008 Olympics

Freestyle riders will have to wait a little longer to compete in the Olympics. Freestyle BMX will likely become an Olympic sport at the 2012 games in London, England.

Flying High

All BMX riders love the thrill of hopping on a bike and flying into the air. However, Mat Hoffman and Kevin Robinson soar just a little higher than the rest.

Both have held the record for highest BMX air. Kevin broke it most recently. In 2005, he rode up a giant **quarterpipe** in New York City's Central Park. He flew into the air, reaching a height of 27 feet (8 m) above the edge of the ramp.

However, Mat is the rider with the most daring stunt of all. He once rode his bike off a 3,200-foot-high (975-m) cliff in Norway, did two backflips, and then glided back down to the ground with a parachute. Even for "The Condor" that was flying high.

Kevin Robinson flies through the air on his bike in Central Park.

The ramp Kevin used in Central Park was 27 feet (8 m) high. Altogether he was 54 feet (16 m) off the ground when he set the world record for highest BMX air.

Mat in action

Mat Hoffman

The Norway cliff jump wasn't Mat's only parachute-BMX trick. One time he rode his bike out of a plane soaring about 16,000 feet (4,877 m) above the ground.

BMX 101

BMXers, whether they are racing or performing tricks, need special equipment and safety gear.

FREESTYLE

RACING

Freestyle Helmet
Keeps your head and face safe during a fall; always wear a helmet when riding

Race Helmet
Protects your head and face; always wear a helmet when riding

Padded Jumpsuit
Protects your entire body

Pads
Keep your knees, elbows, and shoulders protected

Pegs
Give you a place to stand during tricks

Brake
Just one, in the back

Gloves
Protect your hands during a fall

Shin Guards
Protect your shins from painful falls

Shoes
For the best protection always wear shoes that completely cover your feet.

Glossary

barspin (BAR-spin) a trick done in the air; the rider spins the handlebars around and grabs them again before landing

Big Air (BIG AIR) a BMX event where riders use huge ramps to launch themselves and their bikes into the air

condor (KON-dur) a large high-flying bird found in North and South America

540 (*five*-FOR-tee) a trick in which the rider makes one and a half spins in the air

flair (FLAIR) a BMX trick that adds a corkscrew-like spin to a backflip

grinding (GRIND-ing) riding along an object and scraping the wheel pegs against the object

halfpipe (HAF-pipe) a U-shaped ramp used for freestyle BMX tricks

heat (HEET) one stage of a multipart race at the end of which the winner gets to advance to the next round

knobby (NOB-ee) having rubber bumps on tires that stick out to grip the dirt

massive (MASS-iv) huge

obstacle (OB-stuh-kuhl) something that blocks a path

quarterpipe (KWOR-tur-pipe) a curved ramp that is one half of a halfpipe

sprint (SPRINT) a short race or section of a race in which riders pedal as fast as they possibly can

tailwhips (TAYL-wips) tricks in which the rider whips the bike around in a circle while keeping the handlebars and his or her own body still

taps (TAPS) when a rider briefly balances one wheel of the bike on an object

vert (VURT) a type of BMX riding that involves riding off a ramp into the air

wiping out (WIPE-ing OUT) crashing

X Games (EKS GAMEZ) an extreme sports competition held every year

Bibliography

Hoffman, Mat. *The Ride of My Life*. New York: HarperEntertainment (2002).

Partland, J. P., and Tony Donaldson. *The World of BMX*. St. Paul, MN: MBI (2003).

Reynolds, Gretchen. "The Games Abridged: BMX Racing." *New York Times* (August 3, 2008).

BMX Plus! magazine

Read More

McClellan, Ray. *BMX Freestyle*. New York: Scholastic (2008).

Peterson, Angie. *BMX Racing*. Mankato, MN: Capstone (2006).

Savage, Jeff. *Dave Mirra*. Minneapolis, MN: Lerner (2007).

Woods, Bob. *Mat Hoffman*. Mankato, MN: Child's World (2006).

Learn More Online

To learn more about BMX's tricks, stars, and competitions, visit
www.bearportpublishing.com/X-moves

Index

Beijing, China 18
Big Air 16
Bohan, Corey 14–15
Central Park 20
Dandois, Matthias 11
Day, Mike 9, 18
Dhers, Daniel 16–17
dirt 10, 14–15
double flair 4–5

flatland 10–11
freestyle 10–11, 12, 14, 16, 19, 22
Hoffman, Mat 12, 20–21
Holley, Eric 14
Kintner, Jill 18
Mirra, Dave 12–13
motocross 6
Norway 20–21

Olympic Games 9, 18–19
park 10, 12, 16–17
Robinson, Donny 18
Robinson, Kevin 4–5, 20
street 10, 14, 16
vert 10, 12–13, 16
X Games 4–5, 16–17